MW01047067

7 STRATEGIC PRAYERS
YOU SHOULD PRAY
WHEN FEELING
DISCOURAGED

Jerry A. Grillo, Jr.

7 Strategic Prayers You Should Pray When Feeling
Discouraged

ISBN
978-0-6158-5626-1
Printed in the United States of America.

TABLE OF CONTENT

INTRODUCTION:

Everybody at some time or another has experienced downtime in their emotions. We all have days when it seems like we can't make it. Yes, even Christians have times when crisis and circumstances get the best of us.

The issue isn't that you get overwhelmed with life, or a crisis or even with your relationships. The issue is this; does the situation get the best of you? When we allow bad times to linger too long in our minds, they become more than just a feeling of defeat. They become a season of discouragement.

Discouragement will make you feel like there is no way out of a given situation. At times anything can make you feel discouraged…a wrong voice, a bad decision, an overly corrective friend or mentor. All these, and even more, can make us feel like why bother.

Discouragement is a problem only known to human beings. If the animal kingdom functioned as humans, they would starve to death. When an animal can't conquer another animal for food or territory, it doesn't sit down and become defeated, depressed or discouraged; it moves on. It gets up, moves on, and finds a place where it can rule and conquer. This is called the *'survival'* mode. Sometimes we need to learn from nature. You will not always win so make up your mind that you are not going to become discouraged but that you will *survive*.

It is inevitable that everyone will get down at some point in their life. I have no doubt that you have experienced being discouraged at times. You may be discouraged this very moment.

The dictionary defines **discouragement** as follows: *"a feeling of despair in the face of obstacles; a state of distraught and loss of a sense of enthusiasm, drive, or courage."*

If we look through the Bible, we can see that discouragement has been in existence since the beginning of all things (Genesis) and can be found in many people throughout the Bible. The devil has learned to attack the minds of people by making them discouraged and ultimately depressed. Depression is the sibling of discouragement. When you find either one housed within your mind, you can most assuredly expect the other to be there or follow soon after. Discouragement's goal is to entrap people and keep them there until they are utterly and completely destroyed. The goal of the enemy is to cast out any hope for change. I have often said this and would like to reiterate it again here:

The difference between hope and despair is the ability to believe in tomorrow.

I am saddened by how many people are walking, living and working around us who are hurting and defeated. They walk through life completely void of the will to try to succeed. To be discouraged means to be deprived of confidence, of hope and the willingness to keep going.

You will never walk through this life and not experience discouragement. It causes a sick feeling in the pit of your stomach. The feelings of apathy and sadness as well as attitudes of bitterness and anger can seep in and out of your life.

I have often been discouraged while trying to pastor and survive through the seasons of my ministry. I can't tell you the times I've walked into my sanctuary - ready to preach, pumped up and confessing faith - only to find at the moment I enter and see so many empties seats, I feel upset and downhearted. I've felt like wanting to turn around and go home. My wife and my staff see the pain and hurt on my face. They see the disappointment in my eyes. In my mind I am fighting a demon that is laughing and prodding me, saying, *"You loser. You're a failure. You can't even fill up your own church. Why would you continue to write books and stay on television? How dare you travel and try to help other pastors when you can't even succeed in your own town."* Many times I've sat on the platform looking over the congregation and wondering what in the world I could be doing wrong. At times I wonder why I'm still here.

Amidst the discouragement and all of the questions of why and how, I know that my life is in God's hands and all I can do is get up and shake off that deep feeling of discouragement and try again.

CHAPTER ONE

SATAN'S MOST DANGEROUS WEAPONS

"Then the people of the land tried to discourage the people of Judah. They troubled them in building, and hired counselors against them to frustrate their purpose…" Ezra 4:4-5 NKJV

Notice that the enemy's focus was to discourage the workers of Judah. This was their weapon, their battle tactic. They were purposed in their hearts to frustrate the minds of the leaders. The enemy's goal was to break their focus, and as a result, weaken their resolve and destroy their purpose. They even hired counselors to rise up against them. Be very laborious in who you decide to talk and listen to during a time of discouragement. They may be sent by the enemy to break you and not build you!

THINGS THAT CAN PRODUCE A FRUSTRATED MIND:

1. **Delayed Promises:** When a promise, or a harvest, doesn't come when you expect it to, it can cause a glitch in the mind that may cause you to think that your promise isn't coming at all. This mind-set begins to create worry, and worry is confidence in the adversary.

2. **Discouragement:** When a promise is delayed, you can begin to enter into a season of discouragement. Look at the word discouragement when it is broken

9

up… ("dis" and "courage").

Discouragement will cause you to lose the courage to believe, to stand and to fight. It takes courage to call order into chaos. Discouragement can develop a mind-set of inadequacy as your identity comes into question and disappointment is birthed.

3. **Disappointment:** This stage produces the downward spiral to the end. Disappointment is when expectation is not fulfilled. Have you ever felt disappointed? What happened to your faith at that moment? It was dying!

4. **Depression:** This is usually the result of being disappointed. Depression can start out minor, but I believe it can turn into a toxic spirit if it is not confronted immediately.

5. **Distraction:** Distractions will change your focus.
   - *Focus reveals what you believe.*
   - *Focus decides direction.*
   - *The battle for your life is over your focus.*
   - *Focus is what the mind decides to concentrate on.*
   - *Focus is what the mind becomes obsessed over.*
   - *Focus will decide what you feel. What you feel determines what you will pursue.*

Now the mind is becoming persuaded that victory is not possible.

Most people are locked into their own perception. At this point, defeat is inevitable. Ultimately, you become what you continue to look at.

Someone once said to me, "What you continue to look at will master you."

The difference in people is what they see. This is why so many are still broke. They keep looking at their budget and their debts instead of where they want to be. I'm not saying that a budget is wrong. However, I am saying to make sure you balance out what you keep looking at. What you keep looking at, you will eventually become. Think about this; why do so many stay sick? All they keep talking about is their pain and their sickness.

The enemy is looking for a door to destroy you. Be very laborious and determined to guard what you say and what you are focused on. This formula works for almost every situation in your life.

6. **Defeat:** The enemy has you right where he wants you. You are convinced that there is no way out. You are persuaded to accept your life as it is instead of fighting everyday to change your life. People who stop changing become defeated. Ignorance is the refusal to change.

7. **Deception:** Prepare your mind to walk in the truth. The easiest thing to do when you are fighting a feeling of defeat and discouragement is to begin to lie to yourself. You may also have to watch others

lying to you. They may try to paint a false picture of reality.

Faith is a decision of the mind that forces everything else to line up to it.

25 THINGS THAT MAY CAUSE DISCOURAGEMENT

1. Fatigue
2. Fear
3. Failure
4. Deferred hope
5. Frustration
6. Illness
7. Age
8. Sin
9. Bad attitude
10. Unforgiveness
11. Rejection from someone you look up to
12. Being overlooked for a promotion
13. Being ignored when trying to explain yourself
14. Having someone disrespect you
15. Financial problems
16. Marital problems
17. Inability to pay your bills
18. Bitterness
19. Disloyalty
20. Religion
21. Delayed harvest
22. Over expectation of others
23. Correction
24. Wrong relationships
25. Wrong decisions

PRAYER ONE

Pray That Your Eyes Of Faith Will Remain Open While Feeling Discouraged, So You Will Be Able To See The Bigger Picture.

It becomes easier to focus on the problem instead of the bigger picture when we go through battles and crisis.

We tend to get caught up in the moment of the crisis rather than looking at the momentum your crisis could create for you. Open your eyes and look to see what your problem may produce once you've conquered it.

AVOID TUNNEL VISION:

Tunnel vision is one of the reasons we lose perspective, and it causes us to be unable to see the bigger picture. Being driven into the cave of discouragement isn't much fun. Many have succumbed to this terrible and dreadful place. Being driven by defeat or discouragement can place you in a cave that could stop your future calling and success.

Let me make this clear. Everyone, no matter how much faith you think you may have, will experience the cave of despair. Those who decide to see the bigger picture and come out of the cave will survive the season of the cave. Those who refuse, die in that cave.

When I use the word 'die' I'm not necessarily meaning that you will stop breathing. What I am saying is that you may become one of those who live life void of becoming what God had pre-ordained you to be. There are so many who wake up everyday in that cave. They go to a job they hate and stay in relationships they know they need to walk out of just because they refuse to stand at the foot of their cave and see the BIGGER PICTURE.

Is that you? Are you discouraged? Are you going through something right now that is forcing you to cut off good people?

DANGER OF NOT SEEING THE BIGGER PICTURE:

1. You start to isolate yourself from those who really want to help. The only reason you don't want to stick around is because you know they are going to tell you something you probably already know or that you don't want to hear.

The sad thing is that change is the only remedy that will heal your discouragement.
- Change of pace
- Change of race
- Change of feelings
- Change of attitude
- Change of friends
- Change of study

2. You will begin to believe your problem is unsolvable. Nothing is impossible with God. You must understand that no matter what you've done or what you're going through, God is able to go through it with you! He is big enough to get you through your pain. Here's a good thought: **CHILL OUT; GOD'S GOING TO WORK IT OUT!**

Rest in the presence of the Lord and have faith that God is going to do everything He can to pull you through your problem. The only thing you have to do is keep seeing the bigger picture.

3. The spirit of apathy becomes evident. You will only focus on the walls of the problem and not the exit from the cave when you are going through discouragement. Look around the cave and all you will see is darkness, gloom and death. The cave will start to turn into your coffin. That's when the mind starts saying, "Why bother?" This is a very dangerous place to be. I don't care how old you are when you experienced your failure or feelings of discouragement. God is able to restore and rebuild all the things you've lost! The only thing that is going to stop your success in your future is for you to continue to hang out in that cave.

That is what apathy is. It is the attitude, or decision, to stop trying. Failure isn't determined by a failed project. It isn't determined because one's efforts have fallen short, nor is it defined by one falling down. Failure is not attached to an individual when they fall, only when they decide not to get up. Apathy is the reason that many decide to stay down and not to get up.

4. You will become unable to see any of your past successes. There is a story in the Bible about a major player, a prophet who had the power with his words to stop the heavens from raining for three years.

At the end of the drought that he prophesied, Elijah had a great victory. He turned the people of God back to their God and away from Baal worship. God, through Elijah, caused fire to come down from heaven and lick up twelve buckets of water that was poured over the altar and the offering that was on it.

He killed all the prophets of Baal and watched a small cloud bring an abundance of rain; not to mention all the other times in his life that God moved through him.

God was very protective of this prophet; yet during one season of discouragement Elijah was ready to throw in the towel. He wanted to die. He couldn't see past his season of discouragement. He lost sight of the bigger picture. *(I Kings Chapter 18)*

It is easy to feel a sense of defeat and to want to give up when people are discouraged. Let me encourage you! No matter what you're going through... no matter what you're feeling...even if things aren't going your way, hang in there and don't give up.

God is not through blessing you. What you've already gotten in life is not all you can have. There is more!

There is more on the way! There is more to your life than what you can see. Stay focused on your future and not on your pain or your disappointments.

PRAYER TWO

Pray That Your Faith Will Continue To Grow Strong While In Your Season of Discouragement

The first thing that comes under attack in a season of defeat and discouragement is the willingness to grow and work your faith.

The enemy is very aware that when you stop growing your faith, you've pretty much given up all of Heaven's resources. Heaven's release over our lives only works through faith.

"Faith is Heaven's currency."

I know that when I'm down and feeling discouraged I start to lose hope.

- *Hope is confidence in your future.*
- *Hope is confidence in your dreams.*
- *Hope is the door that faith travels through. Without hope, faith has no vehicle to work through.*
- *Hope is the dream of faith.*
- *Believing is the key that unlocks the door of hope so that faith can create your miracle.*

I remember one time when I was really going through something. I was sitting in my house all alone when I decided to turn on the television. My good friend, Todd Coontz, was on. He looked into the camera and said just what I needed to hear for my faith to increase and my discouragement to dissipate.

"Work your faith... Seasons change!"

Hell knows that when faith stops working, Heaven stops sending. When Heaven stops opening over our lives, the next season you will experience is drought and famine. Discouragement robs us of our ability to continue to believe. Without hope... without faith... without the key to open heaven... guess what? **Hell wins!**

Pray that you will continue to work your faith during these down and hurtful seasons. Let me say it again. Everyone will have seasons where discouragement is all around them, no matter who they are. Don't let anyone try to tell you in the religious arena that if you're saved you shouldn't feel discouraged. That is wishful thinking but it is just not reality. We will all experience train wrecks, defeats and disappointments that create seasons where we want to stop trying. Nevertheless, during these times *work your faith* because faith changes seasons!

When I was a youth pastor serving in the church, God was really moving in our youth services. The church had very few youth attending when I took the position, but we started experiencing a move of God within weeks. Growth was inevitable and we began to grow quickly. This particular church had been around for a long time, a *very long* time.

The deacons and older crowd became annoyed

with the zeal and fervor of the youth and their spiritual hunger. They didn't want the young people sitting up front. They didn't like for them to be radical and praise God loudly and with passion. Now I realize why they objected so strongly. Those old, religious people didn't want to be reminded of how cold and dead their praise had become.

God was moving in such a crazy way in our youth services. Young people were bringing their friends of all races. We were experiencing a multi-cultural youth group. Well, those old, dead religious saints had a fit. They were so angry that within months they called me in and fired me. Let me be truthful. They didn't fire me per say. They just made me quit. I was so hurt and angry. I could not believe how these people were acting.

Oh, and did I mention this was my first youth ministry position since I had gone through a divorce? Years later, after God restored me to Himself, He opened the doors for me to get back to my calling with my new wife. If God calls you, trust me. He will find a way to get you back to your calling.

Here I was back in the ministry and within six months, I was kicked out again; not because of a divorce or a problem, but because God was moving and making religious people nervous. After I left that ministry, God immediately opened another door for me. Let me add this. When I resigned in that church, they asked me to take the new youth with me. Now can you believe that? ...and I did!

In the next church, my wife and I begin to experience an even greater out- pouring of God's power. God was moving even stronger and youth were coming in faster than you could imagine. The place we were ministering at was in a little country town in Alabama; Midland City, Alabama, to be exact.

After some time, the once dark and lifeless parking lot was full of youth and children. When we first began, the Wednesday night service was dead and lifeless. The parking lot was empty and there was no sound of children or youth anywhere. However, life began to spring up all around. Youth and children were all around playing and laughing. It was obvious this church was about to explode in growth.

One Wednesday night I was standing in the parking lot admiring all of the youth that were now attending the church, when the side door opened to the sanctuary and the Pastor walked out. The look on his face was one of defeat and frustration. I asked him, *"Wow! Was it a rough Deacon's meeting tonight or what?"* He looked at me with tears in his eyes and said, *"Yes it was. Tonight they voted to release you and your wife as Youth Pastors."*

I could hardly believe my ears! *"Are you kidding?"* was my only reply. *"No, they don't like all the different kind of young people that are now hanging around the church. They are uncomfortable with their radical change."* I stood there as time began to slow down and my world slowly began to crumble around me. *"This can't be happening to me. I didn't seek coming back to ministry... God sought me out... They asked me to come here."* Little by little, I could feel my spirit diving into the cave of discouragement, apathy and despair. I was falling into the same cave as Elijah.

I seemed helpless to stop it. I went home and my only thoughts were of how crazy the whole situation was. I began to ask myself, *"Why bother?"* I was ready to quit, but then the phone rang and it was a pastor in the area calling to ask me to meet with him. He was about two years younger than I was. I agreed to meet with him and after lunch, he asked me, *"Do you have a problem submitting to someone younger than yourself?"* I said, *"Not if he's called to bring change and allows me to do what I do best, which would be to build a radical youth group."* He said, *"I will not hold you back. If you come, I will give you full empowerment."*

Well, you guessed it. I went and I built a youth group from seven kids to one hundred strong. We became the talk of the city. We were in the local high schools...on local television...playing, preaching and ministering all over the state of Alabama. The church grew to over 400 in just a matter of a few years.

Let me just add this. The board that was there when I arrived began to buck and fuss about the change, but this pastor stood his ground. He did what he said he would do. He allowed the old troublemakers to leave. He never wavered in allowing the youth to become what God wanted them to become: **Soldiers of the Light!** All I can say is, Praise God!

Don't let discouragement stop you! Be faithful...build your faith...don't become weary in well doing, for you will reap in due season if you just don't quit.

Work your faith... faith works!
Work your faith... seasons change!

You have to have your faith to get out. Hebrews says, *"Without faith it is impossible to please God."*

PRAYER THREE

Pray That You Don't Lose Your Fight For Life While Feeling Discouraged

A ship is safe in harbor, but that's not what ships are for."
William Shed

The most dangerous place to be, in a season of discouragement, is the place where you lose the desire to keep fighting. The season you are living in becomes permanent when the sense of fighting fades.

I was sitting in a conference in Dallas, Texas, and the speaker made a statement that I've never heard before. This statement shot faith back into my heart:

"Battle Is The Seed For Territory."

When the children of Israel were heading to the Promised Land, God never spoke to them about the enemy, nor did He ever discuss their battle plans for entry. God only spoke of the provision and blessing the land would provide.

Joseph had a dream that God had given him; it was a brief moment when Joseph looked into his future, to see what He would become. God shows us our future but never our journey. He will let you see a brief picture of what is to come, but never show you the battle you will live through, or the pain and the

23

problems you will have to encounter along the path to your dreams.

The only way you will qualify for your future is to stand up in your season of discouragement and continue to fight for your future.

Pray hard and long over this prayer. When the time comes, if you are unwilling to fight, you will lose the harvest of your dreams. Battle will be your seed for ownership... for control... for reward. Battle is the seed for territory.

It's easy to see the giants in your life such as the mountains, the critics, the skeptics, the doubters, and to want to give up. When the children of Israel refused to enter the Promised Land because there was an enemy, God led them back into bondage. This bondage wasn't one they could pray their way out of. God had now become their chains. He became the source that held them in the wilderness.

Their unwillingness to fight cost them their lives. They all died in the wilderness. Why? They would not sow the seed of battle.

The proof that you belong in a certain place or in a certain lifestyle will be your willingness to fight for it. Battle is the proof that you believe that you belong. If you lose the faith to fight, you may lose your faith forever.

David was able to enter the palace and marry the daughter of King Saul because he was willing to fight. While the whole army hid behind the rock of fear, David decided to face the giant, attempt to change his present life and move into his ordained life. Battle was his seed. He was willing to sow the seed of battle. Battle was the seed for his next season.

There were many who could have entered the palace that day. The only qualification was to face the enemy and be willing to fight. Think how many people you know who are living a meaningless life. The only reason that they are is that they fear change. They won't decide to fight; fight for change, fight for more. They have bought into a life of false humility, thinking that the will of God is for them to be happy with what they have and never think that they could possibly have more. Don't live the life of mediocrity; live the life of plenty.

Don't let your season of discouragement rob you of your courage to face the giant in your life. The battle you face today is the door to your future tomorrow.

Stand! Fight! Win!

Never lose your willingness to fight. Without a battle, there can be no winning or way to prove that you've overcome your crisis. You must stay in the battle to win the war.

Weapons that will be effective in your battle:

1. ***Remember that your weapons are not of flesh.*** Through God you have the power to pull down all strongholds, and that includes discouragement. (2 Corinthians 10:4)
2. ***Speak the Word of God and not words of discouragement.*** For the word of God is a sharp, two edged sword. It is quick and it is powerful. It is so powerful it will pierce the very

25

armor of hell and it will judge the hearts intent. (Hebrews 4:12)

3. ***Your conversation should reflect the mind of a winner no matter how you feel.*** Death and life are in the power of the tongue. Those who love it shall eat the fruit of it. (Proverbs 18:21)

4. ***Take authority over your mind and over Satan, in the name of Jesus!*** The name of the Lord is a strong tower: the righteous run in and they are safe. (Proverbs 18:10) (Philippians 2:9,10)

5. ***Clothe your mind in your spiritual armor by*** putting on the whole armor of God every single day.

6. ***Use the power of prayer and fasting.***

7. ***Pursue and extract the wisdom of a spiritual mentor.***

PRAYER FOUR

Pray That You Will Continue To Believe In Your Purpose

"The way you get meaning into your life is to devote yourself to loving others, devote yourself to your community around you and devote yourself to creating something that gives you purpose and meaning."
Mitch Albom

During times of feeling down, or discouragement, you begin to lose focus of your purpose. Without purpose, life becomes meaningless. The enemy knows that when he can create seasons of discouragement, he can actually detour and detain your very reason for being.

I know when you're feeling down that it's hard to stay glued to your purpose. I promise you this that if you will pray this prayer, the Holy Spirit will help you to stay close to your purpose.

Purpose Gives Life Meaning:

Your purpose is actually what you are here to do. Some may call it destiny; others may call it your assignment. Whatever you want to call it, without purpose, you will wander through life without meaning.

27

3 LEVELS OF MOTIVATION:

1. FEAR: Fear is definitely a motivator. Fear can cause someone to make a decision. The problem with using fear as a motivator is that it doesn't give meaning to what you are motivated to do. Fear causes people to respond, but their decision to act usually fades as soon as the fear is gone.

I witnessed many young people get saved when I was a youth pastor. Those who came to the altar, or to God, by way of fear never seemed to last. The church has used fear tactics for a long time. Many have come to resent this "scary" gospel about hell and demons. I don't believe that fear is a great motivator because it is not a lasting motivator.

2. REWARDS: Many have moved from motivating by fear to motivating with the gospel of prosperity, the gospel of rewards. This is also a motivator. I do believe in the gospel of prosperity. In my opinion, anyone who doesn't believe that God desires for all of His children to be blessed and have more, has a hint of Lucifer in them.

The prosperity gospel has been wrongly attacked. However, let me interject that being motivated by rewards alone can be dangerous. Motivating by rewards may be better and last longer than fear, but this message alone will pan out and fade in times of crisis.

Those who are motivated by rewards only, usually become disheartened when there is a delay on a certain reward. The word reward may also be called harvest, increase or blessings.

Let me add here a personal comment. The law of three applies here; the law of thirty, sixty and one-hundred fold return or increase. I believe that fear is only a thirty-fold way to motivate. Reward is better and at least increases us to a sixty-fold anointing to be motivated to change.

So what happens when reward doesn't come? Harvest will eventually come if you are sowing seed, but many who experience delay will give up or dig up their seed. So reward may motivate, but sometimes it won't last in times of drought, loss and pain. The best way to be motivated is what this prayer is all about.

3. Purpose: When you are motivated by purpose, you are going to last in times of trouble. All the disciples in the past, even those who were martyred, stayed true to their convictions because they were motivated by purpose. How did those who had been through so much last in times of trouble? They did not love their life as their own.

"And they overcame him by the blood of the Lamb and by the word of their testimony, and they did not love their lives to the death."   *Revelation 12:11-12 NKJV*

Notice the last part of this verse. *"They did not love their lives to the death."* How could they do this? They had purpose.

Purpose gives meaning to our lives and adds power to our faith in times of discouragement.

David used the word "cause" when attempting to talk the armies of Israel into fighting Goliath. *David* *said, "What have I done now? Is there not a **cause**?" (1 Samuel 17:29-30 NKJV)* David was letting those around him know that he was fighting, but not because of fear. He wasn't just going to face Goliath because of the rewards that were promised by King Saul. He was going to face the giant because the giant had insulted his God and God's people. He moved into battle because he found purpose in it.

Don't lose sight of your purpose. Pray in times of discouragement that you will maintain the real reason why you are attempting to do what you are doing.

"Where Purpose isn't known, abuse is inevitable."

This is a powerful key. When you lose sight of your purpose, abuse to your life is inevitable. This key applies for almost anything in our lives.

When we don't know the purpose of our spouse, we abuse them.

When we don't understand the purpose of our bodies and health, we abuse our bodies.

When we don't know the purpose of our church, we abuse our church.

When a teenager doesn't understand the purpose of school, they spend their life in school abusing the time that they have to learn, time they can never again regain.

Pray that you will never lose sight of your purpose. Your purpose will sustain you during seasons of discouragement! Ask the Holy Spirit to reveal your purpose to you today if you are unsure of what you have been placed on this earth to do.

PRAYER FIVE

Pray That God Will Give You The Wisdom And Power To Swiftly Silence Wrong Voices

The worst thing you can do is hang around negative and critical people when going through a time of discouragement. The feelings of discouragement are real and the enemy would like nothing more than to put someone around you that will influence you to stop trying.

These people are jealous of what God has placed in you... your anointing... your assignment. They don't want you to survive this season. They appear to be your friends, but they will be the voice that distracts you from your destiny in the end.

I continue to teach my congregation at **The Favor Center** not to counsel with their friends when they are experiencing times of defeat and trouble. Why, you may be thinking? Because most of the time your friends aren't qualified to help you through your pain. Your friends are those around you who can comfort you in a crisis, but few friends can mentor you through them. Your mentors are trained not to leave you the way they found you. They are the voices in your life that have you reaching for more...for higher places.

31

Wrong voices can destroy you immediately. Whoever has your ear has control over your future. Guard your ear with caution. The next voice you hear after you've entered a crisis could be the voice that keeps you there for a long time. Be very laborious to know the voice of the Holy Spirit.

Pray that the Holy Spirit will give you the wisdom necessary to survive to thrive through this season. While you're in this season, attempt to make no major decisions until you have come out of the wilderness of depression and discouragement. I pray that you will always seek the Holy Spirit for wisdom in any given situation.

Imagine what Eve could have missed if she would have only silenced the serpent when it spoke to her in the garden. Think for a moment, as soon as the serpent began to question her about God's instruction, it should have been a clue to her that he wasn't about promoting her through, but driving her out of God's promise and presence.

This will be a very important key for us to learn. We have to learn how to discern who is of God and who is of their own agenda, when speaking to us, while we are going through a battle.

My ears are too fertile to allow anyone to sow seeds of wrong words into them. Your ear is the spiritual reproductive organ in the body of Christ. Wrong words will birth illegitimate seasons in our future if we listen.

Shut down your ears and your mind to those who are complaining about your church, about your pastor or about your change. Run from those who always have a word for you from God. I have had the worst experiences from those kinds of people. They seem to always hear God saying this or saying that, but when it comes down to it, they really haven't heard anything from God. They just heard their own mind speaking.

Do not give your ear to these kinds of people. Protect your mind. Protect your faith. How does faith work? It works through hearing the Word of God. Satan knows that when you are discouraged, you are vulnerable. Some people say that any word is better than silence in times of trouble. This is a myth. It is really better to sit in silence than to have people speaking to you all the time. In fact, while you are speaking, or others are speaking, God is not speaking.

I know this book is about seven prayers, but let me offer this prayer in conjunction to prayer five:

Pray that God Will Surround You with Someone Who Possesses the Spirit of Encouragement and Not a Spirit of Rebuke

The last thing you need when you are down is someone rebuking and preaching to you. You need someone who cares enough to tell you that you are going to win and that you are going to make it. No matter how hard it appears, you will come out victorious!

PRAYER SIX

Pray That You Will Never Get In Agreement To Your Crisis.

"Again I say to you that if two of you agree on earth concerning anything that they ask, it will be done for them by My Father in heaven. For where two or three are gathered together in My name, I am there in the midst of them." Matthew 18:19-20NKJV

Agreement is a powerful law on the earth. It can be very easy to become so engrossed in the pain that you are unable to see the healing during seasons of discouragement. Many times, I have almost succumbed to the problem by allowing my mind to believe that there was no way out. This is how the enemy wins. He doesn't defeat us; we defeat ourselves.

Agreement is one of the most powerful and most overlooked laws on the earth. Notice the verse I opened with, *"If any two of you agree on earth concerning anything..."* This works with people and with crisis. You will begin to build a wall around you that causes you to become boxed into your own discouragement, when you begin to believe in the pain. As a result, you can see no way out. You come into agreement with your plight! This gives discouragement the ammunition it needs to take you out.

I've almost fallen many times in ministry because of ignoring this law, when walking into a sanctuary, seeing empty chairs when I expected them to be full. I have had to over look the empty chairs and see the power of my purpose. I've had to pray this prayer more than once. My wife has seen the sign in my eyes that I was failing in my hope and faith over what God has called me to do.

Most church folks are not the best at helping preachers through their times of discouragement. Most of the time, they will just pack up, quit, leave and never even look back, not caring if you survived the season of defeat and pain. I could give you story after story of people who have walked out on me when I needed them the most. Your mind begins to work overtime when this happens and if you're not careful, you will begin to meditate on those who are leaving instead of what you are here on the earth to do. Trust in the Lord... not in man.

"Some trust in chariots, and some in horses; But we will remember the name of the Lord our God. They have bowed down and fallen; But we have risen and stand upright." Psalms 20:7-8 NKJV

If you can't trust God, then whom can you trust? If you won't believe in God's leaders, then whom will you believe in?

Don't get in agreement to your season of discouragement. When you do, the crisis may win.

Agreement is so powerful. When we line ourselves up with our problem, the problem now becomes our prison. God never intended the problems in life to consume and take us over. He wanted us to learn from them and use them to our advantage, not our defeat. God uses pain, loss and defeat to sharpen our sword of faith. I believe that God knows that when we come out of the wilderness alive, we will no longer fear the enemy and what He can do to us. Thus, the problem becomes the tool we use to survive the next crisis or pain. We are destined to win!

"And let us not grow weary while doing good, for in due season we shall reap if we do not lose heart. Therefore, as we have opportunity, let us do good to all, especially to those who are of the household of faith." Galatians 6:9-10 NKJV

I added this verse here because the promise to us in the house of faith is victory in the end. Don't become discouraged and weary. Weariness means to become faint in heart. Don't lose your passion in times of delayment. Even though it seems like you've been waiting a long time, stay in agreement to your future and not to your crisis. Make sure you continue to do good to everyone. Never allow the season of discouragement to control how you treat and interact with others. This is a necessary instruction. We tend to withdraw from others and allow depression to seep in when we are discouraged. This causes us to start mistreating those we love by pushing them away.

The key to your faith is that in due season you will reap. Reaping isn't an option; waiting in faith is. If we stay the course and not grow faint in heart... faint in faith... faint in our praise... just stay the course... stay in agreement to the promise, then we are going to reap! We are going to experience the good of the land.

"If you are willing and obedient, You shall eat the good of the land; But if you refuse and rebel, You shall be devoured by the sword"; For the mouth of the Lord has spoken." Isaiah 1:19-20 NKJV

Let me let you in on a secret. While I am writing this book, my heart is heavy. I am in a position of waiting for my harvest. My mind becomes tormented over why it's taking so long... I'm watching my children grow up... I spend hours writing... have finished many books... still waiting for God to open doors for me. I want to be clear; I'm not sitting on a couch waiting. I'm doing everything I can to keep swinging the axe. My faith is in the law of eventuality. The key is if I keep swinging and if I believe in my future, then the tree of success will eventually fall.

I remember watching a man swing a sledgehammer on a slab of concrete for what seemed like hours, helping build the house next door to mine. I walked over and asked him why he kept swinging that heavy hammer when it appeared the concrete was not breaking. He looked at me with sweat dripping down his face and said, "The key to winning over this concrete slab is to keep swinging. Don't look at the concrete because it can be deceiving. It appears on the surface that I am not making any headway and that the concrete is absorbing my blows and won't break. However, what you can't see is that inside the slab the concrete is weakening with every blow and eventually it will crack up in pieces."

The law of eventuality is at work in most things in life. That is why Paul said, *"Don't become weary."* Your efforts are not in vain. Your faith is working. It is like a sledgehammer beating on the concrete of success or your miracle. Just because you can't see it on the surface doesn't mean the concrete is not weakening with every blow of faith and expectation.

Just keep swinging...just keep believing... just keep trying and in the end, know that you are going to reap if you do not faint.

I have to hear this for myself just as much as you do. While I am writing, I am still swinging. Let's not quit now. We've come too far and lived too long to give up now. Together we are going to win! If you have fallen, then I add another prayer to this one:

I Pray That You Will Have the Courage to Always Try Again.

PRAYER SEVEN

Pray That You Will Always Remain In An Attitude of Thankfulness

The first thing that usually goes when one is feeling the weight of depression and produces a mind of discouragement is an attitude of thankfulness.

It's hard to stay grateful and thankful when you're feeling like someone or something has disappointed you. Sometimes life is a shipwreck. As a matter of fact, every human alive, at one time or another, has had to survive a shipwreck. When you find your life's ship sinking, you're going to have to step into the lifeboat for a season. Learn how to keep your mind in a state of joy and sing praises.

Keep your heart grateful for the lifeboat while watching the ship in the horizon sink.

This is a key prayer to maintain during sad times. The prayer to stay grateful keeps the mind of judgment and the heart from blaming others, in times of feeling discouraged. It's easy to look around in these times and become unthankful and ungrateful.

An unthankful life will become an un-favored life by God. You can't walk in God's favor with a heart that is ungrateful.

41

Every moment may not be good, but there is something good in everyday.

Guard your heart and mind from becoming a faultfinder, while feeling down. Be cautious not to become argumentative and picky in hurtful times. Things that you would normally overlook may not be as easy to ignore when you're feeling discouraged. This causes you to become a faultfinder and see faults you would not have seen if you weren't walking in this season of discouragement.

Let us live life and be thankful, for if we didn't learn a lot today, at least we learned a little. If we didn't learn a little, at least we didn't get sick, and if we got sick, at least we didn't die. So let us all be thankful. This is a mind-set to maintain in troubled times.

We read in Psalms 100:4 that we are to enter His gates with thanksgiving and into God's courts with praise. You are now close enough to request your needs when you enter the Holy of Holies. This verse sounds great, but we also must understand the New Testament book of Galatians and Hebrews, especially the fourth chapter of Hebrews, where it says we don't have to keep working for God's audience.

"Let us therefore be diligent to enter that rest, lest anyone fall according to the same example of disobedience. For the word of God is living and powerful, and sharper than any two-edged sword, piercing even to the division of soul and spirit, and of joints and marrow, and is a discerner of the thoughts and intents of the heart. And there is no creature

hidden from His sight, but all things are naked and open to the eyes of Him to whom we must give account. Seeing then that we have a great High Priest who has passed through the heavens, Jesus the Son of God, let us hold fast our confession. For we do not have a High Priest who cannot sympathize with our weaknesses, but was in all points tempted as we are, yet without sin.

"Let us therefore come boldly to the throne of grace that we may obtain mercy and find grace to help in time of need." *Hebrews 4:11-16 NKJV*

Notice that the last part says that we can come boldly into His presence and receive grace and help in time of need. The New Testament concept is that we wake up in His presence through Christ. We have immediate access to the throne of God because of Jesus. We don't have to work our way in; that was Old Testament. Thus we must understand that when we wake up in the mornings, we wake up in His presence. We are not working our way through the efforts of thanksgiving and praise to get close to God. We are actually working our way out of His presence into our everyday life. We end up walking through praise and living a life of being thankful. This is my right no matter how discouraged I feel. I will not allow my crisis, my problems or my disappointments to rob me from this right to be grateful and thankful.

It is easy to lose your focus and become unthankful in the times when you feel discouraged. You begin to focus only on the things that have disappointed you or the people who have let you down. You become blind to the things around you that really are going your way.

"In every thing give thanks: for this is the will of God in Christ Jesus concerning you." 1 Thessalonians 5:18

"I thank God for my handicaps for, through them, I have found myself, my work and my God!" Helen Keller

There are times when what is hindering us or trying to hurt us, is the very ingredient that God uses to promote us. God's intention isn't for the storm to discourage you, but to build your faith. It is supposed to cause you to keep believing... to keep trying... to keep hoping.

When discouragement becomes our focus, we become so angry and disappointed that we start hating life, start having an attitude and become very cynical and critical towards other things in our lives.

I have done this so many times. I have allowed something in my life that wasn't going right to affect my praise which in turn affected my attitude, and my attitude affected my heart. As a result, it caused me to become unthankful for all the things that were going right.

Your point of view will always determine your viewpoint.

Let me explain. If I allow my circumstances to

decide my elevation in life, then I may never see past my mountain. Everyone faces mountains. The mountains we face may be financial, relational and perceptional. They may even be mental or spiritual. Whatever mountain you are facing, you have to decide how you're going to handle it. Some may just sit in front of their mountain and cry, others may pray and some may scream words of faith. No matter what your reaction, most of the time, the mountain doesn't move. I know what you're thinking. Doesn't the Bible say that if you speak to your mountain and not doubt in your heart that it will remove itself? Yes, it does, but I believe that sometimes speaking isn't enough.

Here's a thought; *why not just climb the mountain instead of sitting there waiting for it to move. By climbing the mountain you begin to elevate your life.*

When you elevate your perspective, you won't stagnate in life. Your perception decides your position in life, not your status.

The enemy's goal is to completely discourage you and in doing so, stop your focus and your faith. This will destroy your perception. Perception is what the mind believes is real. Perception isn't necessarily the truth, but in your mind it's your truth. I have witnessed so many in the church that think they are living the truth because their perception is distorted. In reality, they are living a lie. Imagine waking up in Heaven and finding out your whole life was a lie. I don't want to end up in that nightmare.

A damaged heart creates a damaged mind.

45

A wounded spirit creates a wounded perception.

The Bible commands us to guard our hearts with all diligence; for out of it are the issues of life (Proverbs 14:12). Let's make a clear understanding about this verse. The word *heart* means mind... and the word *issue* is interpreted as *boundaries*. Guard your mind, because out of your mind are the boundaries you will live by. You and I are walled into our perceptions. I have witnessed so many living beneath what God has set up for us through covenant rights.

God never intended for us to live beneath the load of debt, nor did He set us up to be desolate and lost. We have been lined up for blessings through the connection of His covenant. What has hindered so many from claiming their covenant promises? Their perceptions!

Discouraged people can build a mind-set of defeat and failure. The truth is that those who are discouraged aren't failing or defeated. They are just feeling a moment of being disconnected from their courageous mind.

Pray that in this state of being you don't become angry and lose your heart of gratefulness and thankfulness.

A thankful heart becomes a favored life.

Closing Thoughts

Remember everyone goes through crisis. Everyone at some point in his or her life will fail. Someone once said that you are either in a crisis, going through a crisis or coming out of a crisis.

Don't allow your mind to become bogged down with the memory of your disappointment.

Please, I know what it is to have your mind weighed down with defeat, failure, disgrace and even pain. I know how easy it is to begin to believe your life is useless and that no matter what you attempt to do, you are nothing. These are lies the enemy feeds us to keep us from walking in the spirit of mercy and grace.

Repentance is the only requirement for mercy.

When we begin to confess our feelings, God is merciful to forgive us of our weaknesses.

No matter what you are going through right now or in the future, remember that God loves you no matter what, and so do we at the Favor Center.

We are a JUDGMENT FREE ZONE!

Expect healing today.
Expect peace today.
Expect change today.

Love you!
Dr. Grillo

May I Invite You To Make Jesus Christ The Lord of Your Life?

The Bible says, *"If you will confess with your mouth the Lord Jesus, and will believe in your heart that God raised Him from the dead, you will be saved. For with the heart man believes unto righteousness; and with the mouth confession is made for salvation."* Romans 10:9, 10

Pray this prayer with me today:
"Dear Jesus, I believe that You died for me and rose again on the third day. I confess to You that I am a sinner. I need Your love and forgiveness. Come into my life, forgive my sins and give me eternal life. I confess You now as my Lord. Thank You for my salvation! I walk in Your peace and joy from this day forward. Amen!"

Signed_____

Date _____

Yes, Dr. Jerry! I made a decision to accept Jesus Christ as my personal Savior today, and I would like to be placed on your mailing list.

Name_____

Address_____

City _____ State _____Zip _____

Phone_____

FAVORED PARTNERSHIP PLAN

Dear Favored Partner, God has brought us together… When we get involved with God's plans, He will get involved with our plans. To accomplish any vision it takes partnership. It takes people like you and me coming together to accomplish the plan of God.

WILL YOU BECOME ONE OF MY FAVORED PARTNERS TO HELP CARRY THE BLESSINGS OF GOD ACROSS THIS NATION?

In doing so, there are three major harvests that you are going to experience...
1. Harvest of Supernatural Favor
2. Harvest for Financial Increase
3. Harvest for Family Restoration

Sit down and write the first check by faith, and if God does not increase you in the next months, you are not obligated to sow the rest. Yes, Dr. Grillo, "I want to be one of your monthly partners. I am coming into agreement with you right now for my Three Miracle Harvests."

Dr. Jerry A. Grillo, Jr.

PARTNERSHIP PLAN:

____**300 Favored Champion Partner:** Yes, Dr. Grillo I want to be one of your Favored Champion Partners of **$42.00 a month**. Involve my seed as one of the 300 who helped Gideon conquer the enemy of lack.

____**70 Favored Elders:** Yes, Dr. Grillo I want to be one of your 70 Favored Elders of **$100.00 a month**. I want to be one of those who will help lift your arms, so that we can win over the enemy of fear and failure.

____**MY Best Seed:** $_____.____ Remember, no seed is too small and all seeds multiply. Seeds of nothing will produce harvests of nothing. Send your best seed today.

Name_____

Address_____

City _____State_____ Zip_____

Phone _____Email _____

Write Your Most Pressing NEED Below!

_____

Cut Out and Mail with Check or Money Order To:
Dr. Jerry Grillo
P.O. Box 3707
Hickory, N.C. 28603
If you desire to use your credit or debit card, you can give online at **www.fogozone.net.**

WATCH DR. GRILLO LIVE ON THE WEB.

To Invite Dr. Grillo to Speak and Teach at Your Next Conference, Church, Leadership Meeting, or to Schedule Him for Television or Radio Interviews,

Write To:
Fogzone Ministries
P.O. Box 3707
Hickory, N.C. 28603

Or Email:
fzm@fogzone.net

Fax Invitation To:
828-325-4877

Or Call:
1-888-Favor-Me (328-6763)

RELEASING THE F.O.G.
FAVOR OF GOD

▌ Dr. Jerry A. Grillo, Jr.
Author, Pastor, and Motivational Speaker

Favor Conferences - Dr. Grillo is able to minister to many during seminars and conferences throughout America and around the world. Dr. Grillo's heart is to help encourage and strengthen Senior Pastors and leaders.

Books - Dr. Grillo has written over twenty -five books including best sellers, "Saved But Damaged," and, "Pray for Rain." Dr. Grillo sows his book, "Daddy God," into Prison Ministries across the country; this book shows the love of God as our Father.

Internet and Television - Dr. Grillo is anointed to impart the wisdom of God on Favor, Overflow and Emotional Healing. Online streaming and television has made it possible for Dr. Grillo to carry this message around the world into homes and lives that he would otherwise not be able to reach.

Dr. Jerry Grillo
STREAMING
Miss your local church service? Watch Dr. Grillo online, and see him LIVE.
Sundays @ 10:30am EST &
Wednesday @ 7:00pm EST

@BISHOPGRILLO

/BISHOPGRILLO

GODSTRONGTV

Join the
FAVORNATION
by texting
FAVORNATION
to "22828"

MEDIA & DESIGNS
FOGZONE PUBLISHING
WWW.FOGZONEDESIGNS.COM

WWW.DRJERRYGRILLO.COM

Made in the USA
Middletown, DE
13 September 2024

60408273R00031